I0191885

Caroline L. Capron Coe

The Charity

Caroline L. Capron Coe

The Charity

ISBN/EAN: 9783743329683

Manufactured in Europe, USA, Canada, Australia, Japa

Cover: Foto ©ninafisch / pixelio.de

Manufactured and distributed by brebook publishing software
(www.brebook.com)

Caroline L. Capron Coe

The Charity

THE

CHARITY "BOOM."

BY THE AUTHOR OF "ME."

"FAITH, HOPE, AND CHARITY:
THE GREATEST OF THESE IS CHARITY."

FAIR EDITION.

PUBLISHED BY THE

HAHNEMANN HOSPITAL FREE BED FUND ASSOCIATION.

1880.

COPYRIGHT BY

TROW'S PRINTING AND BOOKBINDING COMPANY,

1880.

Dedicated

TO

THE LADIES OF THE HAHNEMANN HOSPITAL

FREE BED FUND

FAIR ASSOCIATION.

EARNEST IN PURPOSE, UNTIRING IN EFFORT,
AND ABOUNDING IN KINDLY
MINISTRATIONS.

GOD AND THE SUFFERING BLESS THEM!

THE

CHARITY "BOOM."

———————◆———————

ON the door-step—in the white light of
the waning Christmas moon,

When the wind shrieked round the cor-
ners and the fires burned low too soon,

When the pavement creaked the echo of
the passer's rapid tread,

Footfalls hastening to the welcome by
the cheerful fireside spread,
And great frosty tear-drops clustered
round the almost human eye
Of the o'erwrought beast of burden,
while in misty circles high
Rose the warm breath from each nostril,
wasting on the chill night air
E'en as life and heart are wasted by
the bleak breath of despair ;—
Crouched a frail form with a basket,
scarce a woman, more than child,
And with crusts from out my basement
strove to sate her hunger wild ;

While above the harsh wind's rattle I

    could catch her bitter moan,

As she pressed her freezing members

    'gainst the cold unfeeling stone.

And I watched her death-numbed features

    ghastly in the pale moon ray—

Ah! the cold creeps in so surely where

    gaunt Hunger leads the way!

But listen! the lips move: "Oh God!

    tell me why

Thy great loving heart is unmoved by

    my cry;

And why was I fashioned thine image
    to bear,

And tossed on this rough world bereft
    of thy care?

Great Father! *my* Father! for I am
    thy child,

How canst thou be deaf to my anguish
    so wild?

I'm starving, I'm friendless, despised and
    forlorn,

All hope from this poor wretched bosom
    is torn!

Can nothing arouse Thee? the last, the
    last cry!

Great Father! Jehovah! *good Christ,*

let me die!"

Bright the coals gleamed on my hearthstone,

gaily waked the Christmas-cheer;

Soft eyes glistened in the gaslight, red

lips breathed in accents dear,

And I clasped my hands and muttered:

"Surely, hope, and faith are vain;

Heaven and very Hell are parted only

by a window-pane!

Is the God-heart less than human, is

    Omnipotence a jest?

Do the faithful feed on falsehood and

    is trust a myth at best?"

Then my fettered spirit shuddered at the

    thoughts within me bred,

As I dared the impious question, stand-

    ing with averted head.

———

That night in a vision an angel came,

And stood by my bedside and breathed

    my name.

Her folded wings on her shoulders were

crossed,

And the floating locks from her forehead

tossed ;

Her features were lit by a heavenly

grace,

But my blood grew chill—'twas the out-

cast's face !

And I shrank with a mortal's dread

amaze

From the piercing search of a spirit's

gaze.

O marvel of living, O mystery of Death,

Immortality born of Life's wasted breath !

" I   am   come   with   a   message," she
    sweetly   said,

"From Him   whom   ye   impiously   dared   to
    upbraid ;

From the Father in Heaven, that Holiest One

Before whom your prayers and reproaches
    have   come.

" ' Remember the poor,'—'twas your bur-
    den each day

As round the home altar ye gathered to
    pray ;

' Remember the poor,' and like incense
    most sweet

Your petition went up to the dear
mercy-seat ;

'Remember the poor,' and the Great
Giver smiled

To answer the thought of His suppliant
child,

And made you his steward commissioned
to bear

The proofs of his love to the children
of Care.

" 'Remember the poor, and He gave you
gold ;

'*Remember the poor*,' 'twas increased ten-
fold ;

'*Remember · the poor*,' and He blessed
your store,

With his choicest gifts it was teeming
o'er ;

'*Remember the poor*,' and the Heavens
bent low

To the heart that was touched by another's woe.

" Now in silver, merchandise, gold and
stocks,

In bonds, notes and liens under ponder-
　　ous locks,

You're hoarding the treasures and still
　　you pray,

'Gracious Father, remember the poor
　　this day!'

Oh, easy of *conscience*, prospered Chris-
　　tian, take care

Lest you hide in your pocket God's an-
　　swer to prayer!

In a basement hard by, a mother to-
　　night

Is watching and praying and stretching
    her sight,

As the shadowy figures flit to and fro

On the sidewalk that edges her window low.

But she listens in vain for the well-known
    tread,

Of the delicate girl who went out for
    bread.

On the hearth-stone the ashes lie cold
    and gray,

The light in its socket has flickered
    away,

And the cold creeps under the coverlet
    thin :

Nature struggles with death —but, *whose*
is the sin?

And greedy reporters jot down for the
press :
" Unclaimed at the Morgue—Verdict---
Case of distress."

Past the rifted cloud and far into the
blue
I earnestly gazed as the angel passed
through.

2

She shaded my eyes with her kindly
      spread wing

From the unrevealed glory of Heaven's
      Great King,

And showed me the treasures laid up
      for me where

The Saviour my mansion had gone to
      prepare ;

Some spiritless ghosts of benevolent
      deeds,

Upon which a chronic self-righteousness
      feeds,

Some petty subscriptions, some clothes
      out of date,

Some coins dropped in church on the
good deacon's plate,

Some soul-uttered vows, an occasional
prayer

Wrung out by temptation, by sorrow or
care,

A few loves unselfish, some aims stripped
of pride,

Accepted because of the Jesus who
died,

And above them all to my horrified
sight,

The crust that was left on my door-step
that night!

Now I care not what quibbling parsons

    may say

Of a genuine Hell in the good old way,

A most exquisite hell for me it would be,

That crust e'en in Heaven to eternally

    see.

Ah! the finance of Heaven is not brok-

    erage bold,

Where men deal upon margins and buy

    without gold,

And upon see-saws live, down or up as

    it may,

And the gains of a lifetime are lost in
  a day.

There the dollar is dollar, a dime is a
  dime,

Payments given at sight and in no case
  on time;

With the oddest results it cannot be de-
  nied,

For whether you multiply, add or di-
  vide,

You will only find—figure it up as you
  may—

That passed to your credit you've given
  away.

" *The yearly reports then* that *publish*
  my name

With laudable numbers attached to the
  same,

My gen'rous subscriptions, my offerings,
  and then——? "

They had their reward—they were seen
  here of men,

And the angels on duty vouchsafe to
  record

Only charities done in the name of the
  Lord.

We have prated of Charity loudly and
  long,

Have harangued the public with lecture
  and song,

We have opened our hearts to its clam-
  orous call,

And done our whole duty at banquet
  and ball;

We have garnered our thousands with
  Tableaux and Fair,

And builded our hospitals high in the
  air,

We have frescoed their walls and have
  polished their floors,

Have widened their halls and embellished
their doors ;

Great beautiful structures commanding and
bold,

But strongly secured with a fastening of
gold,

Which mocks at the penniless mendi-
cant's cry,

And stifles his plea with an " if" or a
" why ; "

While free circulation, ten times in a
score,

Is checked by red tape if one gets
through the door.

A minute too old or a fortnight too
young ;

The wound of the lip should be one
of the tongue ;

The hump is of muscle, it should be
of bone ;

The cough has a nasal, not bronchial
tone ;

Acute inflammation affected the larynx,

This hospital treats only ills of the
pharynx ;

'Tis a carpal instead of a tarsal strain ;

'Tis a ruptured nerve not a varicose
vein ;

2*

That the adipose touches the heart may
   be seen,
Unfortunate creature, we doctor the
   spleen.
The left limb is fractured instead of the
   right;
You suffer at evening, we treat in day-
   light.

The lid of your eye, 'twere better the
   ball;
The liver at fault, we attend to the
   gall.

'Tis the upper instead of the lower
face ;

An ulna instead of a radius case.

We cancerous affections a specialty
make,

This inclines a polypous nature to
take,—

Till symptoms are made a distinction so
fine

That a vertebra fails to suggest the spine.

And hence the close sieve of a medical
view

Not one in a hundred poor creatures
get through ;

And like good resolutions, a pitiful
horde,

These are laid by at last on a Hospital Board.

And so the great mass of the suffering
poor

Only find under ground an infallible
cure.

Or if to cold sect regulations take
heed,

There is nothing so harsh as an unfeel-
ing creed,

And this rigidly strict diagnostical sight

Is eclipsed by an orthodox stringency quite.

The holiest intentions, unfolding, are
chilled

By "doctrinal points" into just souls
instilled;

And the poles of the magnet most faith-
fully tell

How sectarian tenets good Christians
repel;

Baptist, Methodist, Quaker, High Church,
and a score,

Each honestly shouting "This way is 'THE
DOOR!'"

Till *the faith* is become an indefinite
    word,

Dependent alone on the *place* where 'tis
    heard.   .

And though not in letter, in spirit 'tis
    true,

The food of the Gentile won't nourish
    the Jew,

Pray, into the Protestant Mission or
    " Home "

How shall the unsanctified Catholic
    come,

While the Sisters of Mercy slight mercy
    can feel

For the heretic sufferer's woe or his
  weal.

So we writhe and we suffer, and perish
  and die,

By the line and the plummet of Bigot-
  ry's eye.

More—churches are mortgaged and missions in debt,

Their current expenses reluctantly met,

While boards of trustees armed with by-
  law and rule,

The zeal of the ardent effectually cool.

In the temple of Faith with its far-
reaching spire,

Its silver-toned organ and matchless-
voiced choir,

Its carpeted aisles and cushion-lined
pews,

Its gorgeous stained windows with soft
blending hues,

Its velvet-laid altars with trappings of
gold

Where rich-surpliced teachers God's les-
sons unfold,

Ye mourn in your broadcloth, your vel-
vet, your lace,

The *lien*-ness which shadows the holiest
place,

Since the Great God looks down and
discerns in the gloom

An incumbrance too great for just
Heaven to assume,

And while at the chancel your vows
you record,

The beggar outside may be nearest the
Lord.

But some men are wiser than most men
believe,

And for their short-comings find glorious
retrieve

In the full consecration to ·Jesus they
make,

Of what through the grave they are pow-
erless to take;

So magnanimous selfishness ceases to
breathe,

Consoled by a generous — "I give and
bequeathe—"

Thus fervently hoping God's plans to
o'ermatch

And forward their treasures by Special
Dispatch;

Or chooses a proud *in memoriam* to
  build

Of granite or marble to charity willed,

Which Administrator or Judge perchance
  may

Decide is *no charity* since it *won't
  pay,*

And the good Book has made it exceed-
  ingly plain,

Bread cast on the waters is gathered
  again.

And in that grand spasm philanthropy
  feels

Producing convulsions of lancers and
    reels,

When the great hearts of beauty and
    opulence break

And pour themselves out for sweet
    Charity's sake,

When tailor and modiste and coiffeur
    combine

Their arts till the human is almost di-
    vine,

And arrayed *comme il faut*, of one beau-
    tiful belle

The value in figures is wondrous to
    tell,

And into the scale of just estimates thrown

Her fair market status will quickly be

shown ;

Not the lady herself—'twould be greatly

unfair

With plain creature comforts her charms

to compare—

But the outfit complete of one genuine belle,

When rated at par, let the honest weights

tell.

The round *tout ensemble* an Avenue

store—

Real Estate at an ebb--would provide, if

    not more.

The jewel confining her rich golden

    braid

Would purchase a butcher's entire stock

    in trade.

The quivering pendant just over her

    heart

Would set up the very best stand in the

    mart,

Green grocer or baker, or name what you

    will,

The weak to refresh or the hungry to

    fill.

While just one short yard of her elegant
lace

Would get up a dinner deserving a
grace.

The dainty trimmed slippers encasing her
feet,

At Baldwin's would furnish a pauper complete.

The glittering solitaire adorning her
ear,

Would pay for a modern-built flat a full
year ;

While necklace and mouchoir, and lastly
the loves

3

Of bangles and bracelets and ten-button
  gloves,

Would light up a home lost in darkness
  before,

And keep the grim wolf from full many
  a door.

And now to this outlay, most generous
  be sure,

A ten dollar. ticket we add for the
  poor ;

But with ushers, bill-posters, *et caeteras*
  and gas,

This amount is reduced to a pittance, alas !

And though the small hours with the revel be filled,

The thousands go empty away from the Guild ;

And by this grand farce 'tis most cleverly shown

How both ends of charity center at home.

Now into the scales toss your purses and needs,

Then toss in your duties and toss in your

    deeds,

Next toss in your faith and against it

    your cares,

And toss in your good works and lastly

    your prayers ;

How curious to notice the odds at the

    ends,

So much on the turn of a pivot de-

    pends.

O ladies ! sweet ladies ! kind ladies and

    true !

Think just for a moment how much you
   can do.

Would ye light up another face sweet as
   your own.

And kindle a heart to the joy ye have
   known ;

Would ye shield from the rude gaze a
   fair faultless form,

And shelter a soul from the world's cruel
   scorn ?

Unglove your soft hands, there are tears
   to be dried,

And pillows to smooth whereon loved
   ones have died ;

And sweet little mouths turning up to be

fed,

And child hearts that flutter and watch

for your tread.

Oh be of one sad home the angel, the

light !

Your name its sweet watchword at morn

and at night.

The spirit on earth of 𝕺𝖚𝖗 𝕱𝖆𝖙𝖍𝖊𝖗 𝖎𝖓

𝕳𝖊𝖆𝖛𝖊𝖓,

Let 𝕳𝖎𝖘 𝖓𝖆𝖒𝖊 𝖇𝖊 𝖍𝖆𝖑𝖑𝖔𝖜𝖊𝖉 for joy you

have given ;

And by your kind deeds make His kingdom
  to come,

So best on this earth shall His sweet
  will be done.

O be of its table the fresh daily bread,

And over the erring your sweet pardon ·
  shed,

And guard from temptation where want
  is the snare,

And rescue from evil some frail child of
  care ;

And so be His power and His great glory
  shown.

Forever and ever by one of His own.

𝕬men, and then dance in your heartiest
way,

For a time is to dance as a time is to
pray ;

And 'twill not be surprising, if heeding
your call,

The angels come down to the Charity
Ball.

But the great Metropolitan spirit is
kind,

Though like pictured Justice the oftenest
blind,

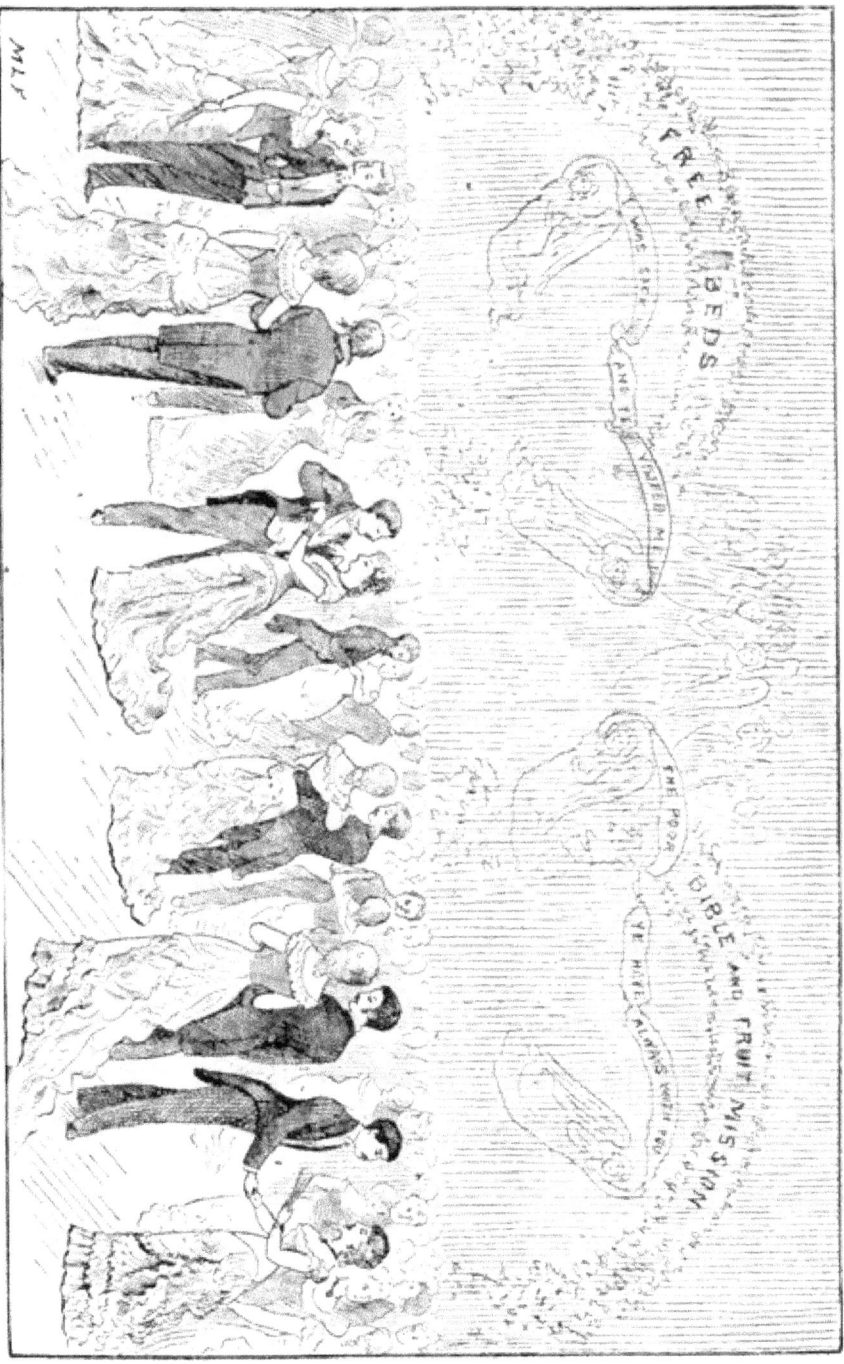

And her holiest thoughts and worthiest
    aims

Are hampered and clogged by invisible
    claims

Of pathies and schisms, of parties and
    power,

Which the rude wheel of Fortune reverses
    each hour.

So she gathers them up, the sick and
    the poor,

The lame and the weary, the mad and
    the sore,

The vile and the hungry, the pauper, the
    thief,

The children of vice, and the victims of

 grief;

So vileness and purity every day ride,

In "corrections and charities" thrown side

 by side;

And kindly removed from the great city's

 din,

The cess-pool of misery she huddles them

 in.

O missions of kind words, of fruits and

 of flowers,

Ye were born of a breath from elysian

bowers.

O sweet loving faces, O delicate tones,

Rich echoes are ye from the heavenly

zones.

O children of mercy, your beautiful hands

Are filling life's hour-glass with glittering

sands,

Whose luminous atoms are catching the

rays

Of beautiful sunlight to measure the

days.

The Heart's-ease that fades on yon suf-

ferer's breast

Is blooming for you in the Land of the

Blest ;

And the whisper of Jesus you breathed

in his ear,

Is the song he shall sing in that holier

sphere.

We travel life's roadway and little we

heed

The God-given power of each thought,

word and deed,

The weight of a smile or the charm of a

tear,

The thrill of a whisper, the chill of a
fear,

The tease of a glance, the check of a
sigh,

The stab of a jest, and the hurt of an
eye.

By the roadway, just there, is a daughter
of shame,

A scar on her conscience, a blot on her
name ;

We loathing, with horror instinctively
shrink

From   lifting   her   fainting   for   only   a

  drink;

But   the   great   heart   of   Jesus   is   moved

  by   her   plea:

"*I*   do   not   condemn"—Are   we   purer

  than   He?

A   father,   a   thief,   hotly   pressed   by   the

  law,

All   eager   her   meshes   about   him   to

  draw;

No   plea   for   his   crime   save   the   echoes

  which   come

From the famishing group in his deso-
late home.

But his free thoughts reach out to the
glad hopes that cling

Round the great Judgment day of an
omniscient King,

That rarest, that richest, that happiest
of days

To the honest with God in his heart
and his ways.

A neighbor, a friend in the days that
have been,

With heart just as loyal, as earnest as
    then,

A bankrupt—what more? Ah, the story
    is old:

Love, friendship and faith even, perish
    with gold.

A child heart is skipping along in the
    way,

Unconsciously sporting with shadows that
    play

Now lengthening, now parting, now
    melting in one

As summery cloudlets coquette with the
  sun ;

A waif on the wide world dropped
  down at your feet—

Oh, the prayer for the fatherless kneel
  and repeat,

And linger a moment, perchance ye may see

Whom the Father will send its *protec-
  tor* to be.

A foot snare—take heed!—in the treach-
  erous sand,

" I am blind, is there any will give me
  a hand !"

I am blind—pity, Lord! only dead eyes can know

How dark is the road the poor sightless must go.

Oh, the struggle with poverty, sorrow, and sin,

Is a struggle in which but the bravest may win,

Though the faint heart must strive and the faltering go

Where the battle is hottest and fiercest the foe.

O ye stalwart of arm and unflinching
of nerve,

Truest heroes are made of the stout
hearts *that serve.*

Pale and dim is the banner protected by
might,

To the *rent* and the *crimson* brought in
from the fight.

The web of God's dealing is wond-
rously spun

With chequers and tracery, shadow and
sun,

And flecked with the atoms of man's
  changeful life,

Which speckle the fabric with turmoil
  and strife;

While spinning and weaving the hum
  of the mill

And buzz of the spindle may never be
  still,

For the warp is set taut and the woof
  of each day

Is filling the shuttle, whose unceasing
  play

Waits neither for tangle, for joy, nor
  for fret,

For prodigal thought nor for useless re-
gret.

But the texture is perfect, come sun-
shine, come gloom,

With man at the spindle and Christ at
the loom.

Oh, pour out your love as God pours
out the showers,

And scatter your smiles as He scatters
the flowers ;

Be the warm breath of truth like their
fragrance distilled,

Till the darkest heart-corners with joy
  shall be filled;
And sprinkle with good deeds life's
  wearisome way,
And pray while you live, and then live
  as you pray!

www.ingramcontent.com/pod-product-compliance
Lightning Source LLC
Chambersburg PA
CBHW032043090426

42733CB00030B/643